SMOKEY from the BLOCK

A CAT COLORING BOOK WITH A CAUSE

The Coloring Saga of a Feral Kitty in New York City

Concept and Story by Laura King

Illustrations by Thomas Draplin

CAUSE COLORING

MW00633554

 **CAUSE COLORING**

© 2017 by Laura King and Thomas Draplin

All rights reserved. Personal photographs were the source materials for these drawings.
The names and likeness of individuals and locations have been changed in some cases to protect privacy. Special thanks to
Dianne Anderson, Dr. Marisa Fuentes, and Dr. Ann Lewis for review. Maria Reyes provided fashion consultation.

SMOKEY from the BLOCK Cat Coloring Book with a Cause is a new work, first published
by CAUSE COLORING in April 2017.

ISBN-13: 978-0692858721
ISBN-10: 0692858725

Printed by CreateSpace.
Manufactured in the United States of America.
Available on Amazon.com and other online stores.

www.causecoloring.com   "Cats Be Cause"

A portion of the net profits from sales of this book will benefit non-profit cat rescue organizations in NYC.

SMOKEY from the BLOCK
CAT COLORING BOOK WITH A CAUSE

WELCOME

Welcome, creative cat lover, to our unique coloring book that is based upon a true and happy animal rescue story. You'll soon have the chance to relax and express your creativity by adding color and your own **pizazz** to the illustrated saga of Smokey, New York City's coolest cat-about-town!

Each illustration within *Smokey from the Block* features the infamous tomcat surrounded by the architecture, fashion, humanity and humor that combine to make New York the world's most vibrant and exciting metropolis. While coloring its streets, you'll succumb to its charm, plus learn more about what you already know and love— CATS! City cats, whether feral or stray, are fascinating creatures that can enrich their neighborhoods and thrive with the help of caring people and progressive city programs. We hope that the coloring journey you take with Smokey will not just fulfill you artistically, but also touch your heart!

WITH YOU IN MIND

[A] On the following printed page, 27 captions enhance Smokey's illustrated story. [B] Since all papers respond differently to various media, we suggest that you explore materials and techniques on the blank end pages of this book before you begin to color. [C] The drawings are printed on single-sided pages and surrounded by a margin that will help you to frame your finished works of art, if you wish. [D] You are our partner in art! Please share your coloring creations and comments with us on Facebook: **Smokey from the Block Cat Coloring Book**, purchase and write a review of this book on **Amazon.com**, and visit our website: **CauseColoring.com** to learn about other cat coloring book projects in progress and our "pawsome" non-profit rescue partners!

OUR INSPIRATION

This coloring project was inspired by the true-life "lost and found" saga of Instagram's **@smokeyfromtheblock** and the experiences of author Laura King as a feral cat caretaker in Harlem. Within NYC's five boroughs, more than 4000 dedicated rescuers to date have been certified to manage city cat populations through a free workshop developed by Alley Cat Allies, the ASPCA and the Mayor's Alliance for NYC Animals (the Alliance). Big respect and raucous cheers for every cat lady and cat guy who rescues 'round New York *and* elsewhere! YOU embody the spirit of compassion and kindness found within these pages.

OUR CAUSE PARTNER

We are excited that a portion of the net profits from sales of *Smokey from the Block* will benefit NYC animal rescue organizations that help stray and feral kitties, including the NYC Feral Cat Initiative, a program of the Alliance: **www.nycferalcat.org.** Check out the last printed page of this book, "A Message from Our Cause Partner," to discover how you can help community cats *wherever* they roam!

CAPTIONS TO THE ILLUSTRATIONS

[Each illustration is numbered in the lower right corner.]

[I] Smokey wanders the streets of Harlem, but this tomcat is not lost. He's street smart and his nose leads him to whatever he's looking for—generally food or lady love and, occasionally, trouble. [2]The great grey tom greets his favorite female friend Mamacita, while her furbabies whisper, "That Smokey cat seems ver-r-ry familiar…" [3]Tough guy Daddy-O Buck is Smokey's fierce rival for Mama's affections. Daddy-O whines a challenge and Smokey throws down a hiss. [4] Caretaker Chiara feeds the colony every day and provides them with warm shelters. [5]Chi is certified by the NYC Feral Cat Initiative to manage the colony and has a plan to TNR (trap-neuter-return) the cats. [6]Once Chi has trapped the cats humanely, they are transported by van to an ASPCA clinic where they are vaccinated and spayed or neutered, then returned back home. The colony kittens are socialized—then, adopted into furever families. [7] All cats that are TNR'd are visually marked by a clipped left ear tip, a badge of honor! [8]The two neutered tomcats are now reformed and stop many of their rude behaviors. Daddy-O Buck remains a loner, but Smokey decides he likes to chill on the sidewalk, calling out to neighbors to collect head pats like bridge tolls. [9] Both males continue to defend their Harlem catdom against marauding members of the Pussy Cat Gang.   [10] Smokey is bitten badly in a clamorous fight over chicken bones. Friends on the block notice his injury and express concern. [11] Smokey's wound swells painfully. He stops eating, and Chi decides he should be seen by a veterinarian. [12] Although ill, Smokey has the strength of a NY Giants linebacker, so Chi recruits a neighbor to help get him into a carrier and a cab. [13]At a 24-hour veterinary clinic, Chi exits the taxi and hoists the heavy carrier up from the back seat. Smokey slides forward, the wire door springs open, and he is catapulted to freedom. [14]Smokey bolts across the street, dodging a sanitation truck. He flees under a line of parked cars toward busy 9th Avenue. [15] Chi quickly loses sight of the cat in the dark. Despairing, she returns home and emails rescue friends to ask for help in finding him. She creates a poster that details the Smokey catastrophe. [16] A rescue team canvases the area, communing with neighbors and stashing cans of tuna in crevices where a frightened cat might hide, but there is no sign of Smokey. Finally, on Day 3, a local spots him from a bench in a park and sends a text to the number on Chi's poster. [17] Chi rushes to the plaza. She calls out for Smokey, and the cat comes to greet her, but when he notices the carrier in her hand, he quickly darts into the bushes. [18] Other rescuers soon arrive with traps and tantalizing treats certain to attract a hungry cat.   [19] Smokey ignores the whole trap-setting commotion—even the sardines and bodega fried chicken. He crawls under an impenetrable hedge and tucks down for a nap. [20] Much later, as night falls and temperatures drop, Smokey stirs and slips past the rescue team onto the shadowy sidewalk. A woman is walking two dogs in his direction, juggling a large cup of coffee. [21] The dogs lurch towards the cat and break free from their owner! Panicking for all his nine lives, Smokey flees down the unfamiliar street. [22] The terrified cat tears into a dead end alley and is cornered. As the dogs close in snapping, a hero appears miraculously and leaps between them! He grabs Smokey by the on-end scruff of his "Big Blue" neck and shields him with his body until the woman can drag her dogs away. [23] The hero recognizes the cat in his arms from the poster. He clenches Smokey tightly against his jacket and heads toward the veterinary hospital. On the way, he collides with wide-eyed rescuers. [24] Chi calls her local vet to arrange an emergency appointment for Smokey. He's examined and prepped for a surgery to repair his ugly wound. [25]After his operation, Smokey is boarded for a few days to recover. The staff is very impressed by Smokey's calm, sociable disposition, and Chi wonders if the grey boy could adapt to apartment living. [26] Many friends from Smokey's block offer their help when they hear his story. Some contribute to his medical expenses, others visit him at the clinic. A neighbor couple offers to foster him, and Smokey is introduced to a new world that includes post-graduate study sessions, soft blankets and food delivery. Things go so smoothly that his new parents "foster fall" and decide to adopt him furever. [27] These days, Smokey's favorite spot is a sunny window ledge where he can spot birds, squirrels and the occasional ear-tipped relative from his former colony. After his legendary ordeal, Smokey is quite satisfied to be an indoor cat with an outdoor view. #

Illustration 1

3

Park closes at
10 PM

CATPHORA

23

CAT ANATOMY

A MESSAGE FROM OUR CAUSE PARTNER

Thank you for supporting Trap-Neuter-Return (TNR) and the New York City Feral Cat Initiative (NYCFCI) with your purchase of CAUSE COLORING's *Smokey from the Block* cat coloring book. The NYCFCI is a program of the Mayor's Alliance for NYC's Animals (Alliance), a private charity.

The NYCFCI helps stray and feral community cats like Smokey and his pals by assisting the efforts of individuals and organizations to care for them and perform TNR. Many community cats are not socialized to humans and are unsuitable for adoption. TNR is the most humane and effective approach to controlling their population and ensuring their best quality of life.

Under the guidelines of the TNR program, community cats are humanely trapped, sterilized, vaccinated against rabies, ear-tipped, and then returned to their outdoor home. TNR results in fewer kittens and less unwanted behavior within a colony, while the cats continue to serve as an ecological rodent deterrent. Neutered cats stay healthier—and they roam less, too. Cats are provided with daily food and warm winter shelters by colony caretakers, who also serve as PR agents to promote a peaceful coexistence between them and their human neighbors.

Feral cats can live long, happy lives in managed outdoor colonies where they stay a safe distance from people. However, sometimes outdoor cats have personality traits that suggest could be happy in a human home. Often these animals are abandoned pets, but sometimes they are street characters like Smokey who just decide over time that they enjoy hanging out with humans. The best thing a colony manager can do is to get to know each cat, and determine its needs as an individual.

The NYCFCI's FREE support services for TNR and colony care include:

- TNR certification workshops in NYC and online
- Specialty training workshops, such as winter shelter building and neighbor relations
- Loans of humane trapping equipment
- Transport to and from spay/neuter clinics via the Alliance's Wheels of Hope van service
- Community outreach materials
- Advice, outreach, public education, and resources via email, phone, and our website

For more information about the NYCFCI and how you can help community cats in your area, please visit **www.NYCferalcat.org**

63355113R00037

Made in the USA
Lexington, KY
04 May 2017